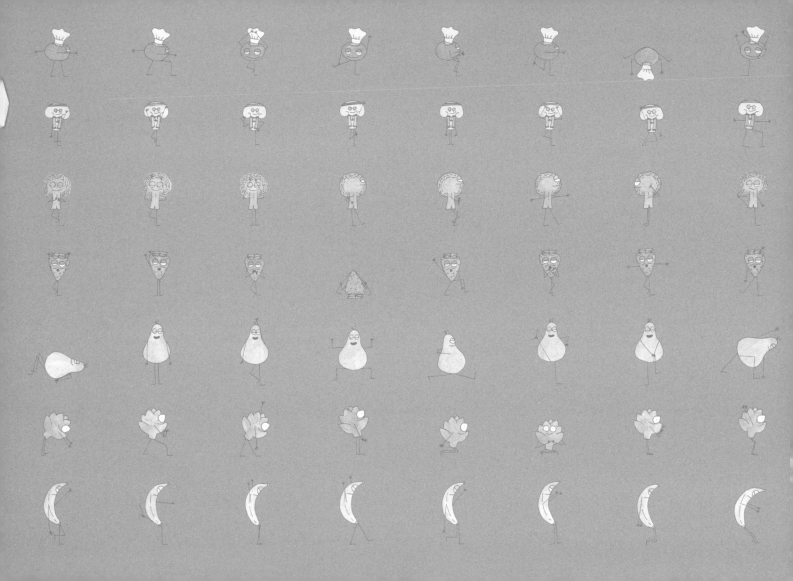

The Vegan Stoner Cookbook

Introduction

In this second cookbook we explore a soy-free menu with fewer processed foods and a focus on whole, natural ingredients.

Soy-based faux meat products are an easy way to get protein in your diet, but some vegans have a soy allergy or avoid soy for other health reasons. Some people stay away from processed foods altogether, and many meat replacers are highly processed. In addition to more than one hundred soy-free recipes, about fifty of the recipes in this book are also gluten-free.

As always, we created simple, easy-to-make, and accessible recipes for stoned vegans or those looking to cook with fewer animal products and more natural ingredients. Substitute freely and have fun cooking!

The Vegan Stoner

Avocado Toast

Serves ◐◐ or ○○○○

Tips
- Top with extra black pepper and adobo seasoning, or try your favorite spice or seasoning.
- Use chopped garlic or other veggies as a topping.

1
Mash an avocado with a fork.

2
Mix the avocado with a handful of nutritional yeast, a few sprinklings of adobo seasoning, and a sprinkling of black pepper.

3
Toast 4 slices of bread.

4
Slice 2 handfuls of cherry tomatoes into halves.

5
Spread the avocado mixture on the toast and top with the cherry tomatoes.

6
Munch.

Banana Porridge

Serves 🥣 or 🥣🥣

Tips
- Add nut milk for a thinner texture.
- Try adding berries (fresh or frozen) and other fruits.
- Oil pan with canola or coconut oil in Step 2.
- Drizzle with chocolate.

1
Peel and mash 3 bananas.

2
Cook the bananas in an oiled pan with a few sprinklings of cinnamon and a few drops of vanilla extract.

3
Mix in a handful of oats.

4
Top with a handful of trail mix.

5
Munch.

Bean Sausage Patties

 Serves   or

Tips

- Replace vital wheat gluten with flour or bread crumbs if necessary.
- Try your favorite legume, like pinto or black beans, instead of kidney beans.
- Use agave in Step 2 if you don't have maple syrup.

KIDNEY BEANS

Stealing Kidneys

Tokes'

LIQUID SMOKE

spice crate

CAYENNE

Sappy Trees'

MAPLE SYRUP

spice bowl

GARLIC SALT

spice tote

THYME

ROB the GLOB

VITAL WHEAT GLUTEN

1
Drain and mash a can of kidney beans in a bowl.

2
Mix the beans with a few drops of liquid smoke and a spoonful of maple syrup.

3
Mix in a few sprinklings of cayenne, garlic salt, and thyme.

4
Mix in 3 spoonfuls of vital wheat gluten.

5
Form patties out of the bean mixture and cook in an oiled pan till brown.

6
Flip and cook other sides till brown, then set aside to cool.

7
Cook 3 handfuls of spinach in the pan with a splash of water and a sprinkling of garlic salt.

8
Munch.

Bean Sopes

Serves ◐ or ◑◑

Tips
- Replace refried beans with any mashed legume.
- Top with blended Aioli 106↗ or Cream Cheese 110↗.

Amazing Corn's
MASA

SWEET WHEAT
WHOLE WHEAT FLOUR

The Chemists
$Na_2CO_3 +$
$2 NaHCO_3$
BAKING SODA

Pepper Villa's
SALSA

spice pail
SALT

spice cap
CUMIN

REFRIED BEANS

1
Preheat oven to 420°F.

2
Mix ½ cup masa flour with ¼ cup whole wheat flour in a bowl.

3
Mix in 3 pinches of baking soda and a few sprinklings of salt.

4
Mix in ½ cup warm water till the dough is moist but still firm. Add more water or masa to adjust if necessary.

5
Mold the dough into cups on an oiled baking sheet. Bake for 9 min.

6
Heat a can of refried beans in a pot, mix in a sprinkling of cumin, then set aside.

7
Cool the sopes and fill with refried beans, some chopped avocado, salsa, and cilantro.

8
Munch.

Beet Smoothie

Serves ☕ or ☕☕

Tips

- Strain for less pulp.
- Replace apple juice with veggie broth for a cold borscht.
- Try your favorite fruit instead of celery.
- Removing the celery leaves and beet tops is optional.

1
Chop a beet, a carrot, and a stalk of celery.

2
Toss the chopped veggies in a blender with 1½ cups apple juice.

3
Blend and serve.

4
Munch.

Blueberry Oat Pancakes

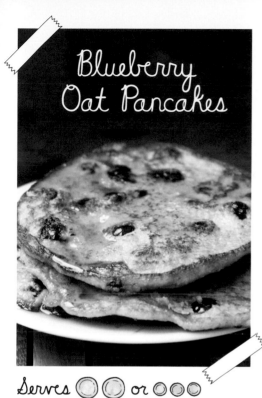

Serves ◯◯ or ◯◯◯

Tips

- Make sure your pan is always well oiled.
- Replace blueberries with trail mix, chocolate chips, or chopped fruit.
- Serve with jam or replace maple syrup with agave.

1
Toss 2 bananas in a blender with 2 cups dry quick rolled oats, 1 cup almond milk, a splash of vanilla extract, and a sprinkling of salt.

2
Blend, then gently stir in 2 handfuls of blueberries.

3
Pour ¼ cup of batter into a hot, well oiled pan and spread out.

4
When the top starts to look dry, flip and cook for the same amount of time, then set aside.

5
Repeat Steps 3 and 4 till the batter is gone.

6
Serve with maple syrup.

7
Munch.

Breakfast Burrito

Serves 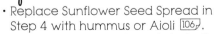 or

Tips
- Replace Sunflower Seed Spread in Step 4 with hummus or Aioli 106.
- Replace broccoli with potato, bell pepper, cauliflower, or your favorite veggies.

 REFRIED BEANS

 HOMEMADE SUNFLOWER SEED SPREAD

 Pepper Villa's SALSA

 Sunny's Gold NUTRITIONAL YEAST

 Flower Power Co FLOUR TORTILLAS

1
Heat a can of refried beans in a pot and set aside.

2
Chop broccoli to make 2 cups.

3
Put the broccoli in a bowl with a splash of water, cover, and microwave for 2 min.

4
Mix some Sunflower Seed Spread 116 with a handful of nutritional yeast.

5
Layer the beans, broccoli, Sunflower Seed Spread, and salsa onto each tortilla.

6
Slice ¼ avocado for each burrito, layer on top of the other ingredients, and roll them up.

7
Heat each side of the burrito in an oiled pan.

8
Munch.

Cauliflower Quiche

Serves

Tips

- Follow package instructions if using store-bought crust.
- Mix in cooked shrooms, bell peppers, or kale.
- If you don't have any veggie broth, replace with water and extra seasonings.

1
Preheat oven to 420°F.

2
Chop a head of cauliflower and a few handfuls of spinach.

3
Toss the cauliflower on an oiled baking sheet with a few sprinklings of garlic salt and bake for 15 min.

4
Remove from oven, flip the cauliflower, add the spinach to the sheet, and bake for 5 more min.

5
Blend the cauliflower in a blender with a handful of nutritional yeast, 1 cup veggie broth, and a few sprinklings of garlic salt.

6
Mix the spinach into the cauliflower mixture, then pour into Pie Crust [112].

7
Bake for 20 min. and let cool.

8
Munch.

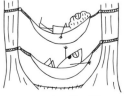

Plantain Rice

Serves ⊙⊙ or ⊙⊙⊙

Tips
- Try adding a few sprinklings of cumin.
- Replace kidney beans with black beans or your favorite legume.
- Toss recipe into a tortilla with avocado and salsa for a quick breakfast burrito.

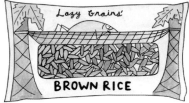

Lazy Grains'
BROWN RICE

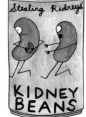

Stealing Kidneys'
KIDNEY BEANS

spice pail
SALT

spice jug
CHILI POWDER

1
Cook ½ cup dry rice.

2
Slice a plantain and ¼ onion.

3
Cook the onion in an oiled pan till browned.

4
Stir in the plantains with a sprinkling of salt and continue cooking.

5
Mix in cooked rice and 1 cup drained kidney beans.

6
Mix in the juice of 1 lime, a few sprinklings of salt, and a few sprinklings of chili powder.

7
Munch.

Potato Hash and Gravy

Serves

Tips

- Add more veggie broth or water it the gravy gets too thick.
- Add cooked onions or thyme in Step 6 for a more flavorful gravy.
- Potatoes can be replaced with your favorite veggie, like carrots or broccoli.

1
Preheat oven to 420°F.

2
Chop a potato and 3 stems of kale.

3
Toss the potato on an oiled baking sheet with a few sprinklings of salt and bake for 20 min.

4
Remove from oven, flip the potatoes, add kale, and bake for 15 more min.

5
Chop a handful of shrooms and 3 cloves of garlic, then cook in an oiled pan.

6
Mix in 1 cup veggie broth, a handful of flour, and a few sprinklings of salt. Stir till thick.

7
Pour gravy over the baked veggies.

8
Munch.

Quinoa Cereal

Serves 🥣 🥣 or 🥣 🥣 🥣

Tips

- Add extra almond milk to taste.
- Sweeten with brown sugar, maple syrup, or chopped bananas.
- Try adding a little coconut oil for texture.
- Try using frozen berries, but be sure to thaw them first.

QUINOA

ALMOND MILK

WALNUTS

BLUEBERRIES

STRAWBERRIES

1
Boil 1 cup almond milk.

2
Stir in ½ cup dry quinoa, turn down the heat, and partially cover the pot.

3
Cook for 15 min., stirring occasionally.

4
Chop a handful of walnuts, a handful of strawberries, and a handful of pitted dates.

5
Stir in the chopped ingredients with a handful of blueberries.

6
Munch.

Strawberry Oat Shake

Serves   or

Tips

- Try adding your favorite fruits.
- Add more nut milk or less banana if you don't like the shake so thick.
- Skip the strawberries and add cocoa powder for a chocolate shake.

1
Cook ¼ cup dry oats.

2
Pour the cooked oats into a blender with 5 strawberries and a peeled banana.

3
Add 1 cup almond milk and 3 pitted dates.

4
Blend till smooth.

5
Munch.

'Tato Migas

Serves 🍽️🍽️

Tips

- Try topping with sliced avocado.
- For faster cooking time, chop potatoes smaller or microwave them first.
- Try adding garlic salt or corn to beans.
- Salsa verde can be replaced with enchilada sauce.

1
Chop 1 potato, a few green onions, and ¼ red onion.

2
Cook the potato and red onion in an oiled pan till soft.

3
Slice 4 Corn Tortillas 109 into strips and mix into pan with ¾ cup salsa verde.

4
Heat a can of drained black beans in a separate pot.

5
Serve migas with beans and top with green onions.

6
Munch.

Walnut Biscotti

Serves  +

Tips

- Replace walnuts with almonds or your favorite nut.
- Bake for an extra couple of minutes in Step 7 for crispier biscotti.
- Try adding a sprinkle of salt in Step 4.

1
Preheat oven to 420°F.

2
Mash ½ banana in a mixing bowl.

3
Mix in ¼ cup canola oil, ¼ cup applesauce, ½ cup brown sugar, and a spoonful of vanilla extract.

4
Mix in 2 cups flour, 1 spoonful of baking powder, and 2 handfuls of chopped walnuts.

5
Knead the dough and divide in half.

6
Form each half into a long roll and lay them on an oiled baking sheet.

7
Press down on the rolls to flatten the tops, bake for 10 min., and let cool.

8
Slice dough into ½ inch slices, then bake for 3 min. on each side.

9
Munch.

Apple Tahini Salad

Serves 🥣 🥣 or 🥣 🥣 🥣

Tips

- Maple syrup can be replaced with brown rice syrup, molasses, or agave.
- Add an extra spoonful of tahini for a creamier texture.
- Try adding dried fruit.

Seed Smuggler's TAHINI

Sappy Trees' MAPLE SYRUP

Flying Legumes' CHICKPEAS

1
Chop a red bell pepper and a green apple and toss in a bowl.

2
Add a spoonful of tahini, a spoonful of lemon juice, and a spoonful of maple syrup.

3
Mix in a can of drained chickpeas.

4
Munch.

Artichoke Bean Salad

Serves

Tips
- Add chopped Seitan 115 for a heartier version.
- Replace sugar with agave.
- Top with Cashew Parmesan 108.
- Toss in chopped bell pepper or celery.

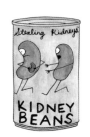

1

Toss ½ can drained white beans and ½ can drained kidney beans in a bowl.

2

Break apart 3 artichoke hearts and toss into the bowl.

3

Mix in 3 spoonfuls of white vinegar, 1 spoonful of olive oil, and 2 spoonfuls of sugar.

4

Serve on chopped spinach and top with black pepper.

5

Munch.

Avocado Walnut Pizza

Serves

Tips

- Use only ½ tomato if large.
- Replace walnuts with almonds, cashews, or your favorite nuts.
- Try adding a leafy green like spinach.
- Use a rice-based tortilla to make this gluten-free.

1

Chop a handful of basil leaves, a tomato, and 3 cloves of garlic.

2

Mash a large avocado in a bowl and mix with the chopped basil and a sprinkling of salt.

3

Cook 2 handfuls of rinsed walnuts in an oiled pan with the chopped garlic and a sprinkling of salt.

4

Remove the walnuts and set aside.

5

Cook both sides of 2 tortillas in the oiled pan till crispy.

6

Remove from the pan and spread the avocado mixture on the tortillas.

7

Top with the chopped tomato and walnuts.

8

Munch.

BBQ Jackfruit Sammies

Half Moon

BURGER BUNS

Serves ◯◯◯

Tips

- Replace the cashews and garlic salt with Aioli 106.
- Sliced pickles or relish make a good addition.

1
Soak 1 cup cashews in hot water for 30 min.

2
Drain and blend the cashews with ½ cup fresh water and a few heavy sprinklings of garlic salt and dill.

3
Grate or thinly slice a carrot and a zucchini, then toss in the bowl with the cashew sauce.

4
Drain and chop a can of jackfruit.

5
Cook the jackfruit in a hot oiled pan.

6
Mash the jackfruit with a fork and mix with ½ cup BBQ Sauce 107.

7
Spoon the cashew veggie slaw and BBQ jackfruit onto buns.

8
Munch.

BBQ Skewers

Serves ◯ ◯

Tips

- Try different combinations of bite-sized veggies.
- You may need to cut skewers to fit your pan. If you don't have skewers, skip Step 4 and serve with toothpicks.

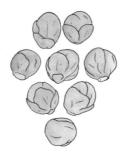

1
Chop ¼ red onion and ½ orange bell pepper.

2
Cut the ends off a handful of Brussels sprouts, toss in a bowl with a splash of water, then microwave for 1 min. to steam.

3
Remove stems from a handful of mushrooms.

4
Alternate mushrooms, onion, cherry tomatoes, bell pepper, and Brussels sprouts on skewers.

5
Cook each side of the skewers in an oiled pan, adding BBQ Sauce 107 as you go.

6
Add a splash of water if the pan goes dry.

7
Munch.

Beet Burger

Serves

Tips

- Use a food processor for Step 2 if you have one.
- Press patties down on a flat surface in Step 5, then use a spatula to move them carefully to the pan.
- You can replace aioli with soy-free veganaise in Step 6.

1
Mix ½ cup falafel mix with ⅓ cup water and let sit for 10 min.

2
Chop 1 cup beets as small as possible.

3
Stir the beets into the falafel mixture.

4
Heat an oiled pan.

5
Carefully form the mixture into 2 patties and cook in the pan till blackened on each side. Flip very carefully.

6
Serve on buns with Aioli 106 and Dill Pickles 111.

7
Munch.

Chive Baked Potato

Serves  or ○○○○

Tips
- Top with more cooked veggies, Seitan 115, or legumes for a heartier version.
- Top with vegan sour cream or hot sauce.

1
Soak 1 cup cashews in hot water for 30 min., then drain.

2
Blend the cashews with ½ cup water, a spoonful of lemon juice, 3 cloves of garlic, and a sprinkling of salt.

3
Poke holes in 2 potatoes with a fork, wrap in wet paper towels, and microwave for 6 min. in a dish.

4
Check the softness with a fork. Large potatoes may need a splash of water and 6 more min.

5
Flip the potatoes and cut out a wedge to make room for cashew sauce.

6
Pour the sauce into each opening and microwave for another minute.

7
Top with a handful of chopped chives and a few chopped cherry tomatoes.

8
Munch.

Eggplant Pasta Salad

Serves  or

Tips
- Replace the eggplant and tomato with your favorite veggies.
- Try with capers instead of pepperoncinis.
- Add more tomatoes if you don't have an eggplant.

1
Cook and drain 2 cups dry fusilli.

2
Chop ½ eggplant and 1 tomato.

3
Cook the eggplant in an oiled pan till soft and browned.

4
Add a drizzle of oil while cooking.

5
Mix in the tomato, ½ cup sliced black olives, and 4 spoonfuls of chopped pepperoncinis with a few sprinklings of garlic salt.

6
Add the veggies to the pasta and mix in 2 spoonfuls of olive oil with 2 spoonfuls of balsamic vinegar and a few sprinklings of garlic salt.

7
Munch.

Jackfruit Toona Salad

Serves

Tips
- Replace the Sunflower Seed Spread with soy-free veganaise or Aioli [106].
- Replace the celery with carrots or your favorite crunchy veggie.
- Add chopped nori for extra ocean flavor.

1
Prepare Sunflower Seed Spread [116].

2
Chop about 2 cups drained jackfruit, 2 stalks of celery, and ¼ red onion.

3
In bowl, mix together the chopped veggies and ½ cup Sunflower Seed Spread.

4
Mix in ¼ cup sliced black olives, 2 spoonfuls of mustard, and a few sprinklings of dill.

5
Mix in 3 spoonfuls of capers and a splash of caper juice.

6
Munch.

Pumpkin Soup

Serves  or

Tips

- Replace the green onion topping with fresh basil, cilantro, or your favorite dried spices.
- Add more water or Cashew Milk 108 for a thinner soup.
- Serve with fresh garlic bread.

PUMPKIN PURÉE — Squashed Squash Co

COCONUT MILK — Hairy Coconuts

WHITE BEANS — Sun Deprived Co

CHILI POWDER — spice jug

CINNAMON — spice can

SALT — spice pail

1
Chop 3 cloves of garlic and cook in an oiled pan.

2
Add a can of pumpkin purée, 1 cup coconut milk, and 1 cup drained white beans.

3
Add a sprinkling of chili powder, a sprinkling of cinnamon, and ½ spoonful of salt.

4
Top with a handful of chopped green onions.

5
Munch.

Red Lentil Stew

Serves 🥣🥣 or 🥣🥣🥣

Tips

- Top with cilantro or paprika.
- Replace water with veg broth in Step 1.
- Try different spice combinations like cinnamon and ginger with coriander, or black pepper and turmeric.

THREE LEGUMES' RED LENTILS

Stacked Olives

OLIVE OIL

spice pail
SALT

spice barrel
PAPRIKA

spice cap
CUMIN

1
Cook 1 cup dry red lentils in 2 cups water and set aside.

2
Chop ½ red onion, 4 cloves of garlic, and 2 tomatoes.

3
Heat 3 spoonfuls of oil in a pot and cook the chopped ingredients with a sprinkling of salt.

4
Mix in the cooked lentils, a spoonful of paprika, and a few sprinklings of cumin.

5
Stir in a few more sprinklings of salt and let simmer for a few min.

6
Munch.

Seitan Gyros

Serves

Tips

- Add a few sprinklings of dill, paprika, or your favorite spices.
- Use store-bought seitan and vegan aioli (sometimes called toum) if you're short on time. Replace the aioli with soy-free veganaise if it's easier to find.

1
Chop 2 handfuls of cherry tomatoes and 2 handfuls of Seitan 115.

2
Cook the seitan in an oiled pan with a few sprinklings of garlic salt and parsley, then set aside.

3
Toast the pita bread and spread with Aioli 106.

4
Top the pitas with the chopped seitan and cherry tomatoes.

5
Sprinkle with parsley and fold in half.

6
Munch.

Seitan Noodle Soup

Serves

Tips

- If you don't have enough broth, use water and a little seasoning.
- Try seasoning with cayenne or your favorite spices.

 **VEGGIE BROTH** (Jumping Onion's)

 celery

 **GARLIC SALT** (spice bowl)

OREGANO (spice cage)

 carrot

BLACK PEPPER (spice goblet)

 **SEITAN** (Rob the Glob's)

 **FUSILLI PASTA** (The Curly Ones)

onion

1
Cook and drain 1½ cups pasta.

2
Chop and cook 2 handfuls of Seitan [115] in an oiled pan and set aside.

3
Chop ¼ onion, a large carrot, and 2 stalks of celery.

4
Cook the veggies in an oiled pot till the onions are slightly brown.

5
Add 4 cups veggie broth and cook the veggies till soft.

6
Stir in seitan and pasta with a few sprinklings of garlic salt.

7
Mix in a few sprinklings of black pepper and oregano.

8
Munch.

Southwestern Quinoa Salad

Serves  +

Tips

- Toss into a tortilla with guacamole and salsa for a quinoa burrito.
- Replace quinoa with different grains like farro or barley.

1
Cook ½ cup dry quinoa in 1 cup water and set aside.

2
Chop a red bell pepper, a jalapeño, and a handful of cilantro.

3
Cook 1 cup of corn in an oiled pan with about 2 cups drained black beans.

4
Mix in the bell pepper and jalapeño, juice of 1 lime, and a few sprinklings of garlic salt.

5
Mix in the quinoa with the veggies in a bowl and top with cilantro.

6
Munch.

Spaghetti Squash Salad

Serves ◯◯

Tips

- Add more water in Step 2 if pan gets dry.
- Add red pepper flakes for spice.
- Try green onions instead of chives.
- Add legumes for more protein.
- If the spaghetti squash is small, cook both halves.

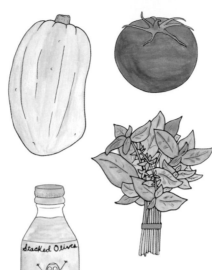

1
Slice a spaghetti squash in half lengthwise and remove the seeds.

2
Place one half of the spaghetti squash in a large pan, cut-side down, with ½ inch (2.5 cm) of water. Steam till soft inside, about 25 min.

3
Let cool, then scrape out the insides with a fork.

4
Chop a tomato, a handful of basil, and a handful of chives.

5
Mix the squash and veggies in a bowl with 2 spoonfuls of olive oil.

6
Mix in a few sprinklings of garlic salt.

7
Munch.

Spanish Rice

Serves ◯◯◯

Tips
- Add to burritos and tacos.
- Try adding oregano, adobo seasoning or cumin.
- Top with cilantro.

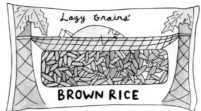

Lazy Grains'
BROWN RICE

Spice Pail
SALT

Spice Jug
CHILI POWDER

Veggies United Co.
FROZEN VEGETABLES

1
Cook 1 cup dry brown rice in 2 cups water and set aside.

2
Chop ½ onion, 2 tomatoes, and 3 cloves of garlic.

3
Cook the chopped onion and garlic in an oiled pan.

4
Add the tomatoes and 1 cup frozen veggies.

5
Mix in the cooked rice, a few sprinklings of salt, and a few sprinklings of chili powder.

6
Munch.

Street Corn

Serves ◯ or ◯◯

Tips

- Replace the aioli in Step 3 with a soy-free veganaise.
- Replace the chili powder with paprika in Steps 3 and 6 for less spice.
- Add red pepper flakes or chili sauce to sauce in Step 3 for more spice.

AIOLI

spice jug
CHILI POWDER

Pepita Pumpkin's
PUMPKIN SEEDS

1
Preheat oven to 420°F.

2
Place 2 ears of corn with husks on a baking sheet, then bake for 30 min.

3
Mix ¼ cup Aioli [106] in a bowl with a sprinkling of chili powder and the juice of ¼ lime.

4
Remove the corn from the oven and let cool.

5
Remove the husks and top with the aioli mixture.

6
Top with cilantro, pumpkin seeds, and more chili powder.

7
Munch.

'Tato Stuffed Peppers

Serves ◎ ◎ or ◎◎◎◎

Tips
- Skip the bell peppers for an easy mashed potato recipe.
- Substitute cauliflower or carrots for the potatoes.
- Skip Step 3 by using instant mashed potatoes.

1
Preheat oven to 420°F.

2
Slice 2 bell peppers in half, discard the seeds and stems, and bake skin-side up for 20 min.

3
Chop 2 potatoes and boil till soft.

4
Drain and mash the potatoes with 3 spoonfuls of olive oil, the juice of ½ lemon, a few sprinklings of garlic salt, and a splash of water as needed.

5
Remove the bell peppers from the oven. Stuff with the potato mixture.

6
Top with a handful of chopped walnuts and a handful of cilantro.

7
Munch.

Tortilla Noodle Salad

Serves ○○

Tips

- Make this recipe gluten-free by using rice-based tortillas.
- Try adding beans for protein.

Pepper Villa's SALSA

Sunny's Gold NUTRITIONAL YEAST

spice bowl GARLIC SALT

Flower Power FLOUR TORTILLAS

1
Chop a zucchini, cook in an oiled pan with garlic salt, then set aside.

2
Slice 3 tortillas into thin strips, cook in the oiled pan, then set aside.

3
Chop ½ avocado and mix in a bowl with 2 spoonfuls of nutritional yeast and a sprinkling of garlic salt.

4
Arrange the cooked veggies on the tortilla strips.

5
Top with salsa and the avocado mixture.

6
Munch.

Walnut Tacos

Serves ◉ or ◎◎

Tips
- Try adding lime juice.
- Serve the mixture in corn or flour tortillas.

1
Chop a handful of walnuts and a handful of sunflower seeds.

2
Heat the chopped nuts in an oiled pan.

3
Add ½ cup corn and 2 spoonfuls of balsamic vinegar.

4
Place the mixture in lettuce leaves.

5
Slice ½ avocado.

6
Top the tacos with avocado slices and salsa.

7
Munch.

Avocado with Cowboy Caviar

Serves ◯ or ◯◯

Tip
• Try adding chopped bell pepper, garlic, or freshly squeezed lime juice.

1
Mix ¼ cup drained black beans with ¼ cup corn in a bowl.

2
Mix in ½ cup Salsa Fresca 112.

3
Mix in a sprinkling of garlic salt and chili powder.

4
Mix in a spoonful of agave.

5
Serve in ripe avocado halves.

6
Munch.

Baba Ghanoush

Serves 🥣🥣 or 🥣🥣🥣

Tips

- If the skin is difficult to peel off in Step 4, scrape out the insides with fork.
- Replace the eggplant with cooked chickpeas.
- Use in lasagna, falafel pie, burritos, or as a sandwich spread.

Spice Pail
SALT

Stacked Olives
OLIVE OIL

Seed Smuggler's
TAHINI

1
Preheat oven to 420°F.

2
Poke holes in 2 small eggplants with a fork and bake till soft, about 35 min.

3
Chop 2 cloves of garlic and a handful of parsley.

4
Peel off the eggplant skin, drain the excess water, and mash the insides with the chopped ingredients.

5
Mix in 2 spoonfuls of tahini, a spoonful of olive oil, a few sprinklings of salt, and the juice of ¼ lemon.

6
Munch.

Butternut-chos

Serves ⬤⬤⬤

Tips
- Use canned butternut squash if necessary.
- Replace jalapeños with pepperoncinis or your favorite chili.

1
Slice a butternut squash in half lengthwise.

2
Remove the seeds and skin from one of the halves.

3
Chop the squash (about 3 cups) and boil in water till soft.

4
Drain and toss in a blender with 2 handfuls of nutritional yeast.

5
Add a few sprinklings of garlic salt, ½ cup veggie broth, and the juice of ¼ lemon.

6
Blend.

7
Pour over chips and top with jalapeño slices.

8
Munch.

Caponata

Serves

Tips
- Serve with toast, crackers, or chips.
- Use in sandwiches, pasta dishes, or salads.
- Tomatoes can be replaced with bell peppers.

Caeser's olives
pitted GREEN OLIVES

Caped Caper's
CAPERS

Spice Pail
SALT

Candy Man's
SUGAR

Rotten Veggies'
WHITE VINEGAR

1
Chop ½ onion, ½ eggplant, ½ cup olives, and 2 tomatoes.

2
Cook the eggplant in an oiled pan with a few sprinklings of salt till soft, then set aside.

3
Cook the onion in the oiled pan with the tomatoes, olives, 2 spoonfuls of vinegar, and 2 spoonfuls of sugar.

4
Mix in 4 spoonfuls of capers and the cooked eggplant.

5
Munch.

Collard Greens

Serves 🍚🍚

Tips
- Add a sprinkling of salt to mellow out the bitterness.
- Try mixing in your favorite veggies.
- Makes a great side with mashed potatoes.

1
Chop ½ onion and 4 cloves of garlic.

2
Remove and chop the leaves from 8 stems of collards.

3
Cook the onion in a pan with 2 spoonfuls of olive oil till browned.

4
Stir the chopped collards and garlic into the pan.

5
Stir in a few sprinklings of cumin, black pepper, and ginger.

6
Munch.

Firecrackers

Serves ◯◯

Tips
- Replace the peanut butter with any nut butter that has a high fat content.
- Try eating just one firecracker to test its potency before eating more.

1
Preheat oven to 420°F.

2
Spread peanut butter on 8 crackers.

3
Grind ½ spoonful of weed (about a teaspoon) and sprinkle onto the crackers.

4
Sandwich the crackers together.

5
Place each sandwich on its own rectangle of foil and seal all edges.

6
Bake for 15 min.

7
Let cool in the foil.

8
Munch.

Green Pea Guac

Serves 🍜 🍜 or 🍜 🍜 🍜

Tips
- Try replacing the bell pepper with tomato.
- Chill in the fridge for about 20 min.
- Add more jalapeño for extra spice.
- Serve with chopped veggies, tortillas, chips, pitas, crackers, or bread.

1
Cook 2 cups frozen peas in an oiled pan with 2 whole cloves of garlic.

2
Chop ½ bell pepper and a handful of cilantro.

3
Chop ½ jalapeño and ¼ red onion.

4
Toss the peas and garlic in a blender with ¼ cup water and the juice of 1 lime.

5
Mix the peas with the chopped veggies and a few sprinklings of salt.

6
Munch.

LOVE AND PEAS CO.
FROZEN PEAS

SALT
spice pail

Hasselback 'Tatoes

Serves ⊙⊙

Tips

- Replace the white bean sauce with Cream Cheese [110].
- Replace the green onions with chives or your favorite veggies.
- Add nutritional yeast to Step 6 for extra cheesy flavor.

1
Preheat oven to 420°F.

2
Cut slits into 2 potatoes without cutting all the way through.

3
Place the potatoes on a baking sheet with the sliced sides facing up.

4
Drizzle olive oil in between the slits.

5
Bake for about 40 min.

6
Blend 1 can drained white beans with the juice of 1 lemon, a spoonful of olive oil, 3 cloves of garlic, ¼ cup water, 2 green onions, and a sprinkling of salt.

7
Pour the mixture over the potatoes, then top with chopped green onion and a sprinkling of cayenne.

8
Munch.

Nooch Nuts

Serves ◯ ◯

Tips

- Try adding a bit of cayenne for spice.
- Replace the almonds with cashews, walnuts, or your favorite nuts.

1
Rinse 2 handfuls of almonds and cook in an oiled pan.

2
Stir and remove from heat when they start to brown.

3
Mix in a few sprinklings of salt and nutritional yeast.

4
Munch.

Peach Salsa

Serves 🥣🥣🥣 or 🥣🥣🥣🥣

Tips
· Add sliced jalapeño or your favorite chili in Step 3 for a spicier version.
· Try adding to sandwiches, tacos, burritos, or curry dishes.

1
Chop ½ red onion, 2 cloves of garlic, a handful of cilantro, and 3 cups of peaches.

2
Cook the onion in an oiled pan till soft.

3
Mix in the peaches, garlic, the juice of ½ lime, a few sprinklings of salt, and a spoonful of vinegar.

4
Remove from the heat, let cool, and mix in the cilantro.

5
Munch.

Red Lentil Mash

Serves 🥣🥣

Tips

- Make a wrap with this and other veggies.
- Use an onion if you don't have a leek.
- Add water or extra veggie broth for an onion-lentil soup.

THREE LEGUMES' RED LENTILS

Jumping Onion's VEGGIE BROTH

spice pail SALT

spice tote THYME

1
Boil 2 cups veggie broth, then add 1 cup dry red lentils.

2
Put on low heat and cover partially.

3
Simmer till mushy, about 20 min., stirring occasionally.

4
Chop 2 cloves of garlic and the tender part of 1 leek.

5
Stir in the garlic, leek, a sprinkling of salt, and a few sprinklings of thyme.

6
Munch.

Roasted Pumpkin Seeds

Serves ◎◎

Tips

- Try seasoning seeds with adobo, black pepper, chili powder, curry powder, or garlic salt.
- Make a sweet version by using coconut oil, cinnamon, and sugar.
- Use other squash seeds instead.

1
Preheat oven to 420°F.

2
Slice a pumpkin in half and remove the seeds.

3
Rinse the seeds with water to remove the pumpkin strings.

4
Toss the seeds in a bowl with 2 spoonfuls of olive oil.

5
Mix in a few sprinklings of salt.

6
Spread the seeds on a greased baking sheet.

7
Bake for 10 min.

8
Munch.

Seasoned Green Beans

Serves 🥣 🥣

Tips
- Slice the bell pepper and green beans to the same length for consistency.
- Try substituting balsamic vinegar for the lemon juice.

AGAVE

SALT

CORIANDER

OLIVE OIL

1
Chop 2 handfuls of green beans, a red bell pepper, and 4 cloves of garlic.

2
Cook the green beans and bell pepper in a pan with 2 spoonfuls of olive oil.

3
Mix in the chopped garlic, juice of ¼ lemon, a drizzle of agave, a few sprinklings of salt, and a few sprinklings of coriander.

4
Munch.

Stuffed Sunflower Tomatoes

Serves

Tip

- Try replacing Sunflower Seed Spread with hummus, Aioli 106↗, or refried beans.

1
Preheat oven to 420°F.

2
Cut the tops off 2 tomatoes and gently remove the insides with a spoon.

3
Mix ½ cup Sunflower Seed Spread 116↗ with 2 spoonfuls of nutritional yeast and a few sprinklings of black pepper.

4
Stuff the tomatoes with the sunflower seed mixture.

5
Place on baking sheet and bake for 20 min.

6
Top with chopped basil leaves.

7
Munch.

Sweet Potato Fries

Serves ⊙ or ⊙⊙

Tips
- Season with other spices like adobo seasoning, garlic salt, or chili powder.
- Make a sweet version with sugar, cinnamon, and a little salt.
- Use Aioli 106↗ as a dipping sauce.

1
Preheat oven to 420°F.

2
Slice a large sweet potato into sticks.

3
Toss on a baking sheet with 2 spoonfuls of olive oil and a few sprinklings of salt.

4
Bake for 20 min.

5
Flip the fries over and bake for 15 more min.

6
Munch.

Tomato Caper Crackers

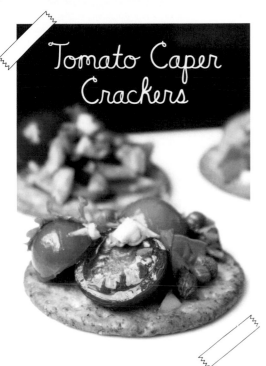

Serves  ⊙⊙ or ⊙⊙⊙

Tips
- Serve on a bagel with Cream Cheese 110 instead of crackers.
- Try using a different leafy green.

1
Slice 2 handfuls of cherry tomatoes in half.

2
Chop a handful of fresh basil and 3 cloves of garlic.

3
Mix the tomatoes, basil, and garlic in a bowl with 3 spoonfuls of capers and 2 spoonfuls of olive oil.

4
Serve on crackers.

5
Munch.

Virgin Spicy Bloody Mary

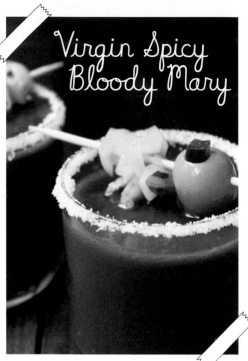

Serves

Tips

- When salting the rim, pour salt on a plate and then rub the glass onto it.
- Pearl onions, celery, and pickles also make good garnishes.
- Add vodka for a nonvirgin version.

1
Pour 1 cup ice in a blender with 2 cups tomato juice.

2
Blend with a spoonful of olive juice, 3 spoonfuls of hot sauce, and the juice of ½ lemon.

3
Rub a lemon wedge around the rim of a glass, then dip the rim in salt.

4
Pour the blended mixture into the glass.

5
Garnish with olives and pepperoncinis.

6
Munch.

White Bean Hummus

Serves 🥣 or 🥣🥣

Tips
- Serve with chopped veggies, bread, crackers, or chips.
- Use in sandwiches, falafel pie, or lasagna.

WHITE BEANS

CUMIN

CAYENNE

GARLIC SALT

TAHINI

OLIVE OIL

1
Heat an oiled pan and toss in 1½ cups drained white beans.

2
Mix in a few sprinklings of cumin, garlic salt, and cayenne.

3
Toss in a blender with the juice of ¼ lemon, a spoonful of tahini, ¼ cup water, and 3 spoonfuls of olive oil.

4
Blend.

5
Munch.

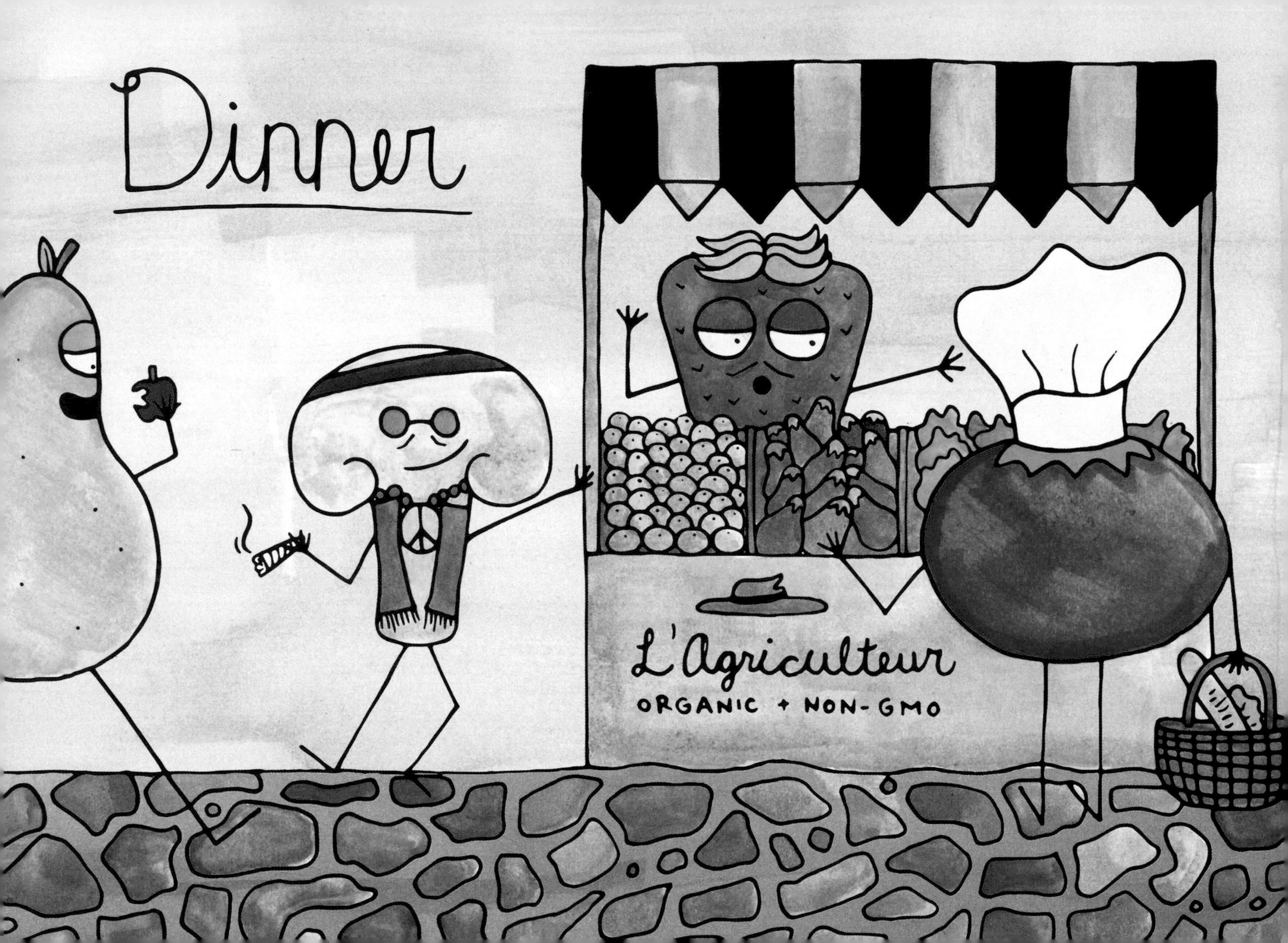
Dinner
L'Agriculteur
ORGANIC + NON-GMO

Buffalo Cauliflower

Serves ⬤⬤⬤

Tips

- Add less water in Step 2 if you want a thick dip. Add more water for a thinner one.
- Replace cashew dip in Steps 1 and 2 with Cream Cheese [110] or Aioli [106].

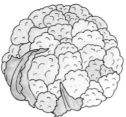

1
Soak 1 cup cashews in hot water for 30 min.

2
Drain and blend the cashews with ½ cup water, the juice of 1 lemon, and a few sprinklings of dill and garlic salt.

3
Preheat oven to 420°F.

4
Chop a head of cauliflower into bite-sized pieces and spread out on an oiled baking sheet.

5
Drizzle olive oil over the cauliflower and bake for 20 min.

6
Remove from the oven, pour hot sauce on top, and bake again for 10 min.

7
Serve the baked cauliflower with the cashew mixture as a dip.

8
Munch.

Cabbage Steak & 'Tatoes

Serves ○○○

Tips
- If you don't have a red cabbage, replace it with a green one.
- Replace potatoes with chopped cauliflower, carrots, or your favorite veggies.

Stacked Olives

OLIVE OIL

Spice Pail
SALT

Spice goblet
BLACK PEPPER

1
Preheat oven to 420°F.

2
Rinse and slice a head of cabbage into 4-6 thick wedges.

3
Chop 2 potatoes and 4 cloves of garlic.

4
Arrange the cabbage and potatoes on large baking pan.

5
Drizzle olive oil over everything, rubbing it into the cabbage to coat evenly.

6
Add a few sprinklings of salt and pepper and bake for 25 min.

7
Flip the roasted veggies, place the garlic pieces on the cabbage, and sprinkle more salt and pepper.

8
Bake 25 more min.

9
Munch.

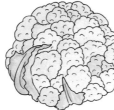

Cauliflower Fondue

Serves ◉◉ or ◉◉◉

Tips

- Replace Brussels sprouts with carrots or your favorite veggies for dipping.
- Replace cauliflower with potatoes or white beans.

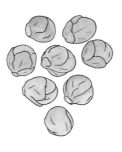
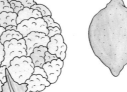

1

Preheat oven to 420°F.

2

Chop a head of cauliflower and slice 2 handfuls of Brussels sprouts into halves.

3

Toss the veggies in oil on a baking sheet and bake for 25 min.

4

Set the sprouts aside, then blend the cauliflower with 1½ cups water, 2 spoonfuls olive oil, 2 handfuls of nutritional yeast, a few sprinklings of garlic salt, and the juice of ½ lemon.

5

Cut out the center of a bread round and chop it into bite-sized pieces.

6

Toast the bread round and bread bites in the oven for about 7 min.

7

Pour the cauliflower mixture into the bread bowl and serve with the sprouts and bread bites.

8

Munch.

Chili Con Corn

Serves

Tips
- Try adding bell pepper, cilantro, jalapeños, or your favorite veggies.
- Mix in some chili powder or red pepper flakes for added spice.
- Add water or veggie broth for a thinner chili.
- Serve with fresh cornbread.

1
Chop ½ onion and 2 tomatoes.

2
Cook the onion in an oiled pot.

3
Drain ½ can kidney beans and ½ can white beans and add to the pot.

4
Add 1 cup corn, ¼ cup BBQ Sauce [107], and the chopped tomatoes.

5
Cover and cook on low for 10 min.

6
Munch.

Coconut Veggie Pasta

Serves ⊙⊙ or ⊙⊙⊙

Tips
- Replace the bell pepper and zucchini with your favorite veggies.
- Try adding chopped nuts in Step 3.
- Try different spices like curry powder, black pepper, chili powder, or paprika.

BOW TIE PASTA

OLIVE OIL

SALT

SHREDDED COCONUT

1
Cook and drain 2 cups dry bow tie pasta.

2
Chop a red bell pepper, 2 small zucchinis, and 3 cloves of garlic.

3
Cook the bell pepper and zucchinis in an oiled pan till soft.

4
Mix in the chopped garlic, a few sprinklings of salt, and a handful of unsweetened coconut shreds.

5
Mix in 2 spoonfuls of olive oil, the cooked pasta, and a few more sprinklings of salt.

6
Munch.

Creamy Broccoli

Serves

Tips

- Use the cream sauce over pasta or vegan burgers, or as a dip.
- Replace the broccoli with your favorite veggies.
- Add cayenne, red pepper flakes, or hot sauce to the blender in Step 6 for extra spice.

WHITE VINEGAR

OLIVE OIL

NUTRITIONAL YEAST

GARLIC SALT

1
Preheat oven to 420°F.

2
Chop 1 potato, 2 cups of carrots, and 2 heads of broccoli (about 4 cups).

3
Throw the chopped veggies on a baking sheet and toss with olive oil.

4
Bake for 25-30 min. and set aside the broccoli.

5
Toss the carrots and potatoes into a blender.

6
Blend with a sprinkling of garlic salt, a spoonful of vinegar, ¼ cup nutritional yeast, and 1½ cups water.

7
Pour the potato-carrot mixture over the broccoli.

8
Munch.

Eggplant Pasta Shells

Serves ◎ ◎

Tips

- Chop the veggies as small as possible so they fit easily into the pasta shells.
- Try adding onion, carrot, spinach, or your favorite veggies.
- Top with fresh basil or parsley.

1

Chop ½ small eggplant, a handful of shrooms, ½ zucchini, and 4 cloves of garlic.

2

Cook the eggplant in an oiled pan with a sprinkling of salt till soft.

3

Stir in the shrooms and zucchini.

4

Stir in the chopped garlic with a spoonful of olive oil and a few sprinklings of salt, then set aside.

5

Cook and drain 8 pasta shells.

6

Stuff the veggies in the shells and top with warmed marinara sauce.

7

Munch.

Jackfruit Tacos

BLACK PEPPER — PAPRIKA — JACKFRUIT

SALSA — BLACK BEANS

Serves

Tips

- Break apart the jackfruit in Step 3 with a fork for better texture.
- Replace black beans with refried beans or your favorite legume.
- Top with cilantro or green onions.

1
Cook a can of drained black beans in an oiled pan with a few sprinklings of black pepper.

2
Spoon the beans into rinsed cabbage leaves.

3
In an oiled pan, cook a can of drained jackfruit with a spoonful of paprika.

4
Spoon the jackfruit onto the tacos.

5
Chop ½ avocado and spoon the pieces onto the tacos.

6
Top with salsa.

7
Munch.

Lasagna Rolls

Serves

Tips

- Replace cashews with mashed white beans, cauliflower, or potatoes.
- Replace spinach with kale or your favorite greens.
- Try adding shrooms or olives in Step 7.

LASAGNA NOODLES

The Royal Carpet Co.

NUTTY NUTS

CASHEWS

Tomato Lovers'

MARINARA

FROZEN SPINACH

CASHEW PARMESAN

Spice Pail

SALT

1
Preheat oven to 420°F.

2
Boil and drain 8 lasagna noodles, then set aside.

3
Soak 1 cup cashews in hot water for 30 min., drain, and toss in a blender.

4
Blend the cashews with 3 cloves of garlic, a few sprinklings of salt, and ½ cup water.

5
Microwave 1½ cups frozen spinach till thawed, about 2 min.

6
Mix spinach into the cashew sauce.

7
Spread the cashew mixture on each lasagna noodle, roll, and place in a baking dish.

8
Top the rolls with marinara and Cashew Parmesan [108] and bake for 12 min.

9
Munch.

Lentil Soup

Serves 🥣🥣 or 🥣🥣🥣

Tips
- Try other spice combinations, such as coriander and cayenne, thyme and parsley, or paprika and turmeric.
- Add more veggie broth for a thinner soup.
- Serve with garlic toast or naan.

The Dental Lentils Co.
GREEN LENTILS

Jumping Onion's
VEGGIE BROTH

spice bowl
GARLIC SALT

spice goblet
BLACK PEPPER

spice cap
CUMIN

1
Cook 1 cup dry green lentils in 2 cups water and set aside.

2
Chop a carrot and ½ onion and cook in an oiled pot.

3
Add 1 cup veggie broth, cover the pot, and simmer till the carrots soften.

4
Add the cooked lentils to the pot with 5 sprinklings of garlic salt and 5 sprinklings of black pepper.

5
Mix in the juice of ¼ lemon and 5 sprinklings of cumin.

6
Munch.

Mac & Squash

Serves 🥣 🥣

Tips

- Removing the skin is optional in Step 2.
- Top with chives or green onions.
- Replace the squash with pumpkin purée or sweet potato purée.
- Replace the water in Step 5 with veggie broth for added flavor.

1
Cook and drain 2 cups dry pasta.

2
Slice an acorn squash in half and remove the seeds from one of the halves.

3
Chop the half squash and boil till soft.

4
Drain and toss the squash in a blender with a spoonful of olive oil and a handful of nutritional yeast.

5
Blend with ¼ cup water, a few sprinklings of garlic salt, and a few sprinklings of paprika.

6
Mix the sauce with the drained pasta and a few more sprinklings of garlic salt and paprika.

7
Munch.

Mushroom Stir Fry

Serves ◎◎ or ◎◎◎

Tips

- Try serving with rice noodles.
- Try a different type of oil as a flavor base.
- Substitute your favorite nuts or seeds for the cashews.

Fun-Guy's CRIMINI MUSHROOMS

Seed Smuggler SESAME OIL

NUTTY NUTS CASHEWS

spice fail SALT

spice basket GINGER

1
Chop ½ onion, 2 handfuls of mushrooms, 3 handfuls of broccoli, a handful of cashews, and 3 cloves of garlic.

2
Cook the onion in a pan with a spoonful of sesame oil.

3
Toss in the rest of the chopped ingredients.

4
Mix in a sprinkling of ginger and a few sprinklings of salt.

5
Munch.

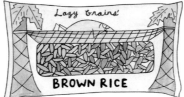

Orange Glazed Veggies

Serves ◎◎

Tips

- Try replacing packaged orange juice with freshly squeezed.
- Orange juice can be replaced with other fruit juices like pineapple.
- Try adding cashews, mushrooms, and chili peppers in Step 4.

BROWN RICE

CORN STARCH

GARLIC SALT

BROWN SUGAR

ORANGE JUICE

1
Cook ½ cup dry rice and set aside.

2
Chop 2 handfuls of broccoli, ½ onion and a bell pepper.

3
Cook the onion in an oiled pan.

4
Mix in the broccoli, bell pepper, and a few sprinklings of garlic salt.

5
Mix 2 spoonfuls of brown sugar in a bowl with ½ cup orange juice, a spoonful of cornstarch, and a few sprinklings of garlic salt.

6
Mix the orange sauce into the pan and stir till the veggies are fully cooked.

7
Serve over the rice.

8
Munch.

Peanut Noodles

Serves  or

Tips

- Try replacing the cayenne with your favorite chili sauce.
- Try adding mushrooms, carrots, or tomatoes.
- Top with avocado slices or cilantro.

RICE NOODLES

Grains in Pain Co.

NUT BUTT COMPANY PEANUT BUTTER

Seed Smuggler SESAME OIL

spice crate CAYENNE

spice lorec GARLIC SALT

spice basket GINGER

1
Cook and drain 2 servings of rice noodles.

2
Chop ½ onion and slice a zucchini into strips.

3
Cook the onion and zucchini in a pan with a spoonful of sesame oil till they start to brown.

4
Mix in ¼ cup peanut butter, ½ cup water, and the juice of 1 lime.

5
Mix in a few sprinklings of garlic salt, ginger, and cayenne.

6
Mix the noodles into the sauce.

7
Munch.

Potato Chowder

Serves 🥣🥣🥣 or 🥣🥣🥣🥣

Tips
- Try replacing the potatoes with cauliflower.
- Reduce the amount of veggie broth for a potato mash.
- Try adding beans or Seitan [115] for more protein.

1
Chop 2 potatoes and ½ head of cabbage.

2
Boil the potatoes in 4 cups veggie broth till soft.

3
Stir in the chopped cabbage, a sprinkling of black pepper, and a few sprinklings of salt.

4
Simmer and stir till the cabbage is soft, about 30 min.

5
Serve with a handful of chopped chives.

6
Munch.

Puttanesca

Serves ◯ ◯

Tips
- Top with Cashew Parmesan 108.
- Try mixing in beans in Step 4 for extra protein.

1
Chop 5 cloves of garlic and 3 tomatoes (or 2 large ones) into small pieces.

2
Simmer the chopped veggies in an oiled pot.

3
Slice ½ cup green olives and mix into the pot.

4
Mix in 2 spoonfuls of capers, a sprinkling of oregano, and a sprinkling of red pepper flakes.

5
Simmer the sauce till most of the water evaporates, about 30 min.

6
Cook and drain 2 servings of pasta, then mix with tomato sauce.

7
Munch.

Red Pepper Gnocchi

Serves

Tip
· Serve this carrot sauce over pasta or your favorite grain.

1
Slice 2 carrots, a red bell pepper, and a jalapeño.

2
Cook the bell pepper and jalapeño in an oiled pan till slightly blackened, then toss in a blender.

3
Boil the carrots in a pot till soft (about 10 min.), set the water aside, and toss the carrots in blender.

4
Cook 4 servings of gnocchi in the boiling carrot water.

5
Blend all the veggies with ½ cup veggie broth, 2 cloves of garlic, and a few sprinklings of salt.

6
Serve the gnocchi with the blended sauce.

7
Munch.

Seitan Pozole

Serves

Tips
- Top with avocado and sliced cabbage.
- Add cooked potatoes for a heartier version.
- Replace seitan with jackfruit for a lighter version.

Rob the Glob's
SEITAN

Jumping Onion's
VEGGIE BROTH

Three Kernels'
HOMINY

Prickly Cactus
ENCHILADA SAUCE

1
Chop ¼ onion and a handful of Seitan 115.

2
Heat a large oiled pot, then cook chopped ingredients till brown.

3
Add 2 cups drained hominy.

4
Add ½ cup enchilada sauce and 2 cups veggie broth, then simmer.

5
Slice a lime and 2 radishes.

6
Serve with radishes, cilantro, and a wedge of lime to squeeze over the soup.

7
Munch.

Seitan Ribs

Serves

Tips

- Serve with potato salad, fries, or cole slaw.
- Add hot sauce or cayenne in Step 5 for a spicier version.
- Peanut butter can be replaced with any nut butter.

ROB the GLOB

VITAL WHEAT GLUTEN

Sunny's Gold

NUTRITIONAL YEAST

spice box

ONION POWDER

spice pail

SALT

spice barrel

PAPRIKA

Colonel Smoke

BBQ SAUCE

NUT BUTT COMPANY

PEANUT BUTTER

Tokes!

LIQUID SMOKE

1
Preheat oven to 420°F.

2
Mix 1 cup vital wheat gluten in a bowl with ½ spoonful of paprika and ½ spoonful of salt.

3
Mix in 2 spoonfuls of nutritional yeast and ½ spoonful of onion powder.

4
Melt 2 spoonfuls of peanut butter in a microwave for at least 30 seconds.

5
Mix the peanut butter into the gluten mixture with ½ spoonful of liquid smoke and ¾ cup water.

6
Knead by hand for a minute, then stretch and flatten into a bread pan.

7
Bake for 25 minutes.

8
Cut into strips and cook in an oiled pan with ½ cup BBQ Sauce 107.

9
Munch.

Shroom Paella

Serves   or

Tips

- Try adding corn, peas, or your favorite veggies for color and nutrients.
- Add saffron or adobo seasoning for flavor.
- Try wrapping in a tortilla with avocado and salsa for a shroom burrito.

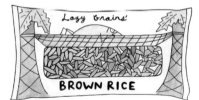

VEGGIE BROTH — CRIMINI MUSHROOMS — WHITE BEANS — ARTICHOKE HEARTS — BROWN RICE — PAPRIKA — GARLIC SALT — ROSEMARY

1
Chop a large tomato (or 2 small ones) and slice 2 handfuls of mushrooms.

2
Cook the tomatoes and shrooms in an oiled pan with a few sprinklings of garlic salt and paprika.

3
Mix in 1 cup drained white beans, 1 cup drained artichoke hearts, and a few sprinklings of rosemary.

4
Mix in ½ cup of dry short-grain brown rice.

5
Pour in 2 cups veggie broth, turn down the heat, and let simmer till the rice absorbs the liquid. Try not to stir.

6
Munch.

Sunflower Pesto

Serves ◯ ◯

Tips

- Replace bow tie pasta with your favorite type of noodles.
- Replace sunflower seeds with your favorite nuts or seeds.
- Use pesto in a sandwich or on crackers.

1
Cook and drain 2 cups dry pasta.

2
Chop 4 cloves of garlic.

3
Cook the garlic in an oiled pan with ½ cup sunflower seeds and a few sprinklings of salt.

4
Toss the garlic and sunflower seeds in a blender with 2 or 3 handfuls of basil.

5
Blend with 3 spoonfuls of olive oil, ½ cup water, and a few more sprinklings of salt.

6
Mix blended sauce with the pasta.

7
Munch.

Sweet Chili Noodles

Serves ○ ○

Tips
- Top with cilantro or green onions.
- You can replace maple syrup with agave.
- Add chili sauce for extra spice.

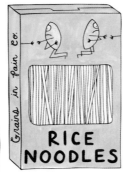

MAPLE SYRUP

RICE NOODLES

COCONUT MILK

SEITAN

GARLIC SALT

CUMIN

CHILI POWDER

1
Cook and drain 2 servings of rice noodles.

2
Chop 2 handfuls of Seitan [115].

3
In a bowl, mix 2 spoonfuls of chili powder, ½ spoonful of garlic salt, and a few sprinklings of cumin.

4
Brown the seitan in an oiled pan, then mix in the spice mixture.

5
Add ½ cup coconut milk and the juice of 1 lime.

6
Mix in the rice noodles and a spoonful of maple syrup.

7
Munch.

Taco Torte

Serves  ○ ○ ○ ○

Tips

- Save time by using riced cauliflower in Step 2.
- Try your favorite combo of veggies instead of corn and cauliflower.
- Top with Sunflower Seed Spread 116 or Cashew Parmesan 108.

REFRIED BEANS

Pepper Villa's SALSA

Happy Trunks' WALNUTS

GARLIC SALT

FLOUR TORTILLAS

1
Preheat oven to 420°F.

2
In an oiled pan, cook 1 cup corn, 1 cup chopped cauliflower, a handful of chopped walnuts, and a few sprinklings of garlic salt.

3
Set aside and heat a can of refried beans in another pot.

4
Oil a pie pan and layer a tortilla, some beans, and some of the corn mixture.

5
Repeat layering the tortillas, beans, and corn mixture two more times.

6
Top with a tortilla and bake for 20 min.

7
In a bowl, mash an avocado with a few spoonfuls of salsa.

8
Top the torte with the avo mixture and a few extra spoonfuls of salsa.

9
Munch.

Tortilla Soup

Serves 🍜🍜

Tips

- Try replacing fresh veggies with salsa if you don't have all the ingredients.
- Try adding corn or beans in Step 3.
- You can replace agave with maple syrup.
- Top with cilantro.
- Add a chipotle pepper for extra spice and flavor.

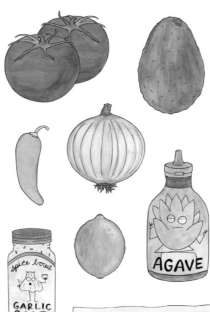

1
Chop 2 tomatoes, ¼ onion, and a jalapeño.

2
Cook the onion in an oiled pot till brown.

3
Stir in the tomatoes, the jalapeño, juice of ½ lime, a spoonful of garlic salt, a spoonful of agave, and ½ spoonful of paprika.

4
Stir in 1 cup water, simmer for about 10 min., then set the pot aside.

5
Slice 2 tortillas into small strips, cook in a hot oiled pan till toasted, and set aside.

6
Serve the soup in bowls and stir in some tortilla strips.

7
Top with a scoop of mashed avocado and more tortilla strips.

8
Munch.

Veggie Fajitas

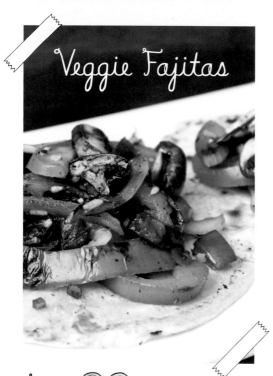

Serves ◯◯

Tips
- Replace the veggies with your favorites.
- Serve with salsa, guacamole, beans, or vegan sour cream.

1
Chop 3 cloves of garlic and a tomato.

2
Slice ½ onion, a green bell pepper, and a handful of mushrooms.

3
In an oiled pan, cook the onion, mushrooms, and bell pepper with a few sprinklings of garlic salt.

4
Mix in the tomato, garlic, and another sprinkling of garlic salt.

5
Cook till soft and set aside.

6
Heat both sides of the tortillas in the oiled pan till browned.

7
Serve the veggies on the tortillas.

8
Munch.

Watermelon Curry

Serves  ⊙⊙ or ⊙⊙⊙

Tips
- Add cayenne for a spicier version.
- Try topping with cilantro or green onions.

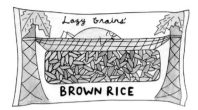
Lazy Grains' BROWN RICE

Spice Kettle CURRY POWDER

Spice Pail SALT

1
Cook 1 cup of dry rice and set aside.

2
Chop 4 cloves of garlic, ½ avocado, and about 4 cups of watermelon.

3
Cook the garlic in an oiled pan with the watermelon and juice of 1 lime.

4
Mix in a spoonful of curry powder and a few sprinklings of salt.

5
Simmer on low heat.

6
Pour the mixture over the rice and top with the avocado.

7
Munch.

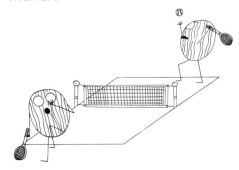

Banana Chocolate Mousse

Serves   or

Tips
- Top with chocolate chips or chopped nuts.
- Try replacing almond milk with coconut milk.

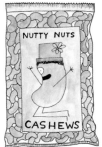

1
Soak 1 cup cashews in hot water for 30 min.

2
Drain the cashews and toss in a blender with 3 bananas.

3
Blend with ¼ cup almond milk, ¼ cup cocoa powder, and 3 spoonfuls of sugar.

4
Munch.

Candied Nuts

Serves 🥣 🥣

Tips
- Be careful cooking sugar on high heat—it can burn easily and stick to the pan.
- Try adding shredded coconut, agave, or more sugar to sweeten.
- Try as a topping on vegan ice cream.

WALNUTS

CASHEWS

SUGAR

ALMONDS

SALT

1
Heat an oiled pan.

2
Toss a handful of walnuts, a handful of cashews, and a handful of almonds in the pan.

3
Mix in a sprinkling of salt and a spoonful of sugar.

4
Stir till the cashews are slightly brown on both sides.

5
Munch.

Cashew Ambrosia Salad

Serves 🥣 🥣 or 🥣 🥣 🥣

Tips

- Replace the coconut milk in Step 2 with oat milk, Cashew Milk 108, or your favorite vegan milk.
- Try replacing agave with maple syrup in Step 2.

1
Soak 1 cup cashews for 2 hours, then drain and toss in blender.

2
Blend with ½ cup coconut milk and 2 spoonfuls of agave.

3
Chop 2 cups of fruit and toss in a bowl.

4
Pour the cashew mixture over the fruit and stir.

5
Top with shredded coconut.

6
Munch.

Coconut Nog

Serves  or.

Tips
- Try adding bourbon or rum.
- Replace almond milk with oat milk, Cashew Milk [108], or your favorite vegan milk.

1
Toss 2 bananas in a blender with 2 cups almond milk.

2
Add ½ cup coconut milk and a spoonful of vanilla extract.

3
Add a few sprinklings of cinnamon, ginger, and nutmeg.

4
Heat the mixture in a pot.

5
Munch.

Fluffy Zucchini Brownies

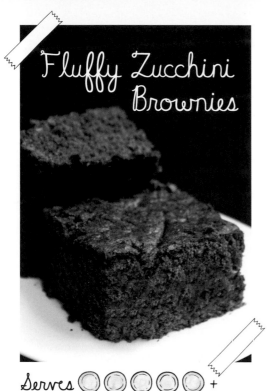

Serves ⊙⊙⊙⊙⊙ +

Tips

- Make this gluten-free by using oat flour, coconut flour, rice flour, almond flour, or your favorite gluten-free flour.
- Try adding shredded coconut, chopped nuts, carob, or chocolate chips in Step 4.

SWEET WHEAT
WHOLE WHEAT FLOUR

Grannie's Cocoa
COCOA POWDER

Coconut Esq.
COCONUT OIL

Sweet Corie's
VANILLA EXTRACT

Spice Pail
SALT

The Chemist
Na₂CO₃⁺
2 NaHCO₃
BAKING SODA

Candy Man's
SUGAR

1
Preheat oven to 420°F.

2
In a bowl, mix 2 cups flour with ½ cup cocoa powder, ½ spoonful of baking soda, and ½ spoonful of salt.

3
Mix in ½ cup melted coconut oil, 1½ cups sugar, ½ spoonful of vanilla extract, and ¾ cup water.

4
Shred 2 cups of zucchini and mix in.

5
Pour in a greased baking pan and bake for 27 min.

6
Munch.

Fruit Compote

Serves 🥣 🥣 or 🥣 🥣 🥣

Tips

- Try using your favorite fruit or making a multilayered version with mixed fruit.
- Try using different flavors of coconut yogurt or other soy-free vegan yogurts.

1
Chop an apple and a pear.

2
Boil the apple and pear in water till soft.

3
Drain the water and toss the cooked fruit in a blender.

4
Blend with a handful of blackberries, the juice of ½ lemon, and 2 spoonfuls of sugar.

5
Serve on top of plain coconut yogurt.

6
Munch.

Fruit Sushi

Serves ◯◯◯

Tips

- Replace these fruits with your favorites.
- Try topping with sesame seeds, coconut milk, or shredded coconut.
- If the rice balls fall apart in Step 6, make a rice bowl with fruit topping.

1
Rinse and drain 1 cup of dry sushi rice till the water isn't so cloudy.

2
Toss the rice into a pot with 1 cup water, ½ cup coconut milk, 2 spoonfuls of sugar, and a sprinkling of salt.

3
Mix once and then do not stir again for the rest of the recipe.

4
Heat uncovered on medium heat till it starts to simmer, then lower heat.

5
Cook till water is gone, about 12 min.

6
Let the rice cool, form rice balls in your palms, then place on a plate.

7
Slice ½ mango, ½ avocado, and ½ grapefruit.

8
Place the sliced fruit on the rice, then top with a few sprinklings of sugar.

9
Munch.

Key Lime Pie

1
Soak 3 cups cashews in water for about 2 hours.

2
Drain and toss the cashews in blender with ¼ cup coconut oil and ⅓ cup agave.

3
Blend with ¾ cup coconut milk and the juice of 4 limes.

4
Pour into a graham cracker crust.

5
Place in the freezer for at least 7 hours.

6
Munch.

Serves ⭘⭘⭘⭘⭘ +

Tips
- Coconut oil can be replaced with canola oil, but the pie won't stay quite as solid.
- Serve with fresh fruit on top.

Peanut Bark

Serves

Tip
• Try adding shredded coconut, chocolate chips, or carob chips.

COCONUT OIL

PEANUT BUTTER

VANILLA EXTRACT

Peanut Muncher Co.

PEANUTS

SALT

The Fainting Cane

POWDERED SUGAR

1
Line a small baking dish with foil.

2
Heat 1 cup peanut butter in a pot on low heat.

3
Mix in ¼ cup coconut oil and stir till well mixed.

4
Mix in 2 sprinklings of salt and a splash of vanilla extract.

5
Mix in 1 cup powdered sugar and 2 handfuls of unsalted peanuts.

6
Spread the mixture into the baking dish and freeze till firm, about 4 hours.

7
Slice into squares.

8
Munch.

Pecan Sandies

Serves ◯◯◯◯◯ +

Tips
- Try replacing vanilla extract with almond extract in Step 3.
- Try using a different nut in Step 4.

COCONUT OIL

WHOLE WHEAT FLOUR

PECANS

SUGAR

POWDERED SUGAR

VANILLA EXTRACT

1
Preheat oven to 420°F.

2
Melt 1 cup coconut oil in a microwave for about 30 seconds.

3
Mix the coconut oil in a bowl with a spoonful of vanilla extract and 3 spoonfuls of water.

4
Mix in 2 ½ cups flour, 1 cup chopped pecans, and ¼ cup plus 2 spoonfuls of sugar.

5
Roll the batter into balls and place on a baking sheet.

6
Bake for 10 min.

7
While warm, roll the balls in a bowl of powdered sugar.

8
Munch.

Polenta Pecan Bites

Serves ◎ ◎

Tips
- Try topping with chocolate chips.
- Try adding a sprinkling of cinnamon or brown sugar.

POLENTA

PECANS

MAPLE SYRUP

SHREDDED COCONUT

1
Slice 4 coins of polenta.

2
Cook the polenta in an oiled pan till brown on both sides, then set aside.

3
Cook a handful of pecans in the oiled pan till the edges darken.

4
Place the pecans on top of the polenta with a drizzle of maple syrup and a sprinkling of coconut shreds.

5
Munch.

Raspberry Bites

Serves

Tips
- Try adding shredded coconut or chopped nuts in Step 3.
- You can replace maple syrup with agave.
- Try dipping in melted chocolate.

Scary Berries' RASPBERRIES

Sweet Cone's VANILLA EXTRACT

Coconut Esq. COCONUT OIL

Spice Jail SALT

Sappy Trees' MAPLE SYRUP

Grannie's Cocoa COCOA POWDER

1
Melt 4 spoonfuls of coconut oil in microwave or heated pan.

2
Mix the oil in a bowl with 2 spoonfuls of maple syrup and a splash of vanilla extract.

3
Mix in 4 spoonfuls of cocoa powder and a sprinkling of salt.

4
Stuff the mixture into raspberry tops.

5
Freeze for about 5 min. to harden.

6
Munch.

Virgin Sangria

Serves

Tips
- Replace the fruit with oranges, grapes, or your favorite fruits.
- Add wine in Step 3, or replace the grape juice with wine in Step 2.

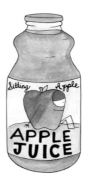

1
Chop a mango, a grapefruit, and a handful of strawberries.

2
Add the chopped fruit to a pot or large bowl with 3 cups grape juice.

3
Add 1 cup apple juice and let the mixture sit in the fridge for at least an hour.

4
Mix in 2 cups sparkling water.

5
Munch.

Watermelon Fresca

Serves 🍵 or 🍵🍵

Tips
- Try replacing strawberries with your favorite berry in Step 1.
- Add a few spoonfuls of sugar for more sweetness.

BERRY STAINED

STRAWBERRIES

1
Toss 3 cups of chopped seedless watermelon in a blender with 1 cup of chopped strawberries.

2
Add ¼ cup water and the juice of 1 lemon.

3
Blend.

4
Munch.

Aioli

Makes 2 Cups

Tips
- Brown the garlic in an oiled pan before blending for added flavor.
- Add fresh herbs, spices, and seasonings to get just the flavor you like.

1
Peel ½ cup garlic cloves.

2
Toss the cloves in a blender with the juice of 1 lemon, ½ spoonful of salt, and ¼ cup cold water.

3
Blend till smooth.

4
Keep the blender on low speed and slowly pour in 1½ cups canola oil.

5
Store in the fridge for up to a week.

BBQ Sauce

Makes 1 Cup

Tips

- Replace the maple syrup with molasses.
- Ketchup can be replaced with blended fresh tomatoes or canned tomatoes.
- Add hot sauce for extra spice.
- Try different types of vinegar for variation.

1

Pour 1 cup ketchup into a bowl.

2

Add a spoonful of liquid smoke and 2 spoonfuls of maple syrup.

3

Add ½ spoonful of cayenne and 4 spoonfuls of vinegar.

4

Add a few sprinklings of garlic salt and black pepper.

5

Mix well and store in the fridge for up to 2 weeks.

Cashew Milk

Makes 3 Cups

1
Soak 1 cup cashews in hot water for 30 min.

2
Drain and blend with 3 cups fresh water.

3
Strain through a cheesecloth into a container.

4
Save cashew pulp for the recipe below.

5
Store in the fridge for up to a week and shake before using.

Cashew Parmesan

Makes 1 Cup

1
Heat 1 cup of cashew pulp from the recipe above in an oiled pan.

2
Mix in 4 spoonfuls of nutritional yeast and a few sprinklings of onion powder and garlic salt.

3
Mix in 2 spoonfuls of olive oil.

4
Store in the fridge in an airtight container for up to a week.

Corn Tortillas

Makes 6 Tortillas

Tip
• See *The Vegan Stoner Cookbook* for our flour tortilla recipe.

1
Mix 1½ cups masa and a few sprinklings of garlic salt in a bowl.

2
Stir in 1 cup hot water and knead the dough.

3
Roll the dough into 6 balls, each about the size of your palm.

4
Flatten out into a desired size using your hands or a rolling pin on a flat surface.

5
Slide a knife or spatula underneath the dough to loosen it from the surface.

6
Cook the tortillas in an oiled pan for about a minute on each side.

7
Munch.

Cream Cheese

Makes 3 Cups

Tips

- Brown the garlic in an oiled pan before blending for added flavor.
- Add fresh herbs, spices, and seasonings to get just the flavor you like.
- For a dessert version, replace the olive oil with coconut oil, and replace the garlic with sugar or maple syrup.

1
Soak 2 cups cashews in hot water for 30 min.

2
Drain the cashews and toss in a blender.

3
Squeeze the juice of 1 lemon into the blender.

4
Add 2 cloves of garlic and ¾ cup water.

5
Add a spoonful of olive oil and a few sprinklings of salt.

6
Blend till smooth and store in the fridge for up to a week.

Dill Pickles

Makes 1 Jar

Tip

- Add fresh herbs and your favorite spices to get just the flavor you like.

1
Chop 4 cloves of garlic and slice a cucumber into spears.

2
Heat 1 cup white vinegar and ½ cup water in a pot on low heat.

3
Mix in 5 sprinklings of salt and the chopped garlic.

4
Mix in a spoonful of dill, 5 sprinklings of black pepper, and 5 sprinklings of cayenne.

5
Let the mixture cool.

6
Place the cucumber spears in a jar and pour in the vinegar mixture.

7
Seal and refrigerate for at least a day.

8
Munch or store in the fridge for up to a month.

Pico de Gallo
(Salsa Fresca)

Makes 2 Cups

1
Chop 2 large tomatoes and ¼ onion, then toss all into a bowl.

2
Chop a jalapeño and a handful of cilantro and mix in.

3
Squeeze the juice of ½ lime into the bowl and stir with a sprinkling of salt.

4
Munch or store in the fridge for up to a week.

Pie Crust

Makes 1 Pie Shell

Tips
- Add a few spoonfuls of sugar for a dessert crust.
- Add garlic powder or dried herbs for a savory crust.

1
Mix 1 cup flour with a pinch of salt.

2
Mix in ¼ cup oil and ¼ cup cold water.

3
Knead into a ball, then roll out into a large circle.

4
Place in a pie dish and poke a few holes in the bottom with a fork.

5
Preheat oven and bake following the recipe instructions.

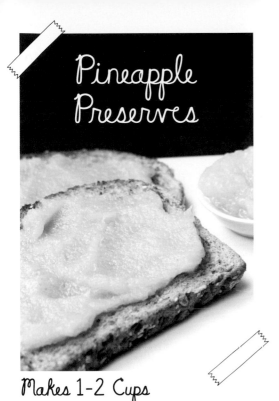

Pineapple Preserves

Makes 1-2 Cups

1
Peel and chop a whole pineapple into chunks (about 4 cups), removing the core.

2
Toss in a blender.

3
Blend till smooth, then pour into a pot.

4
Mix in ½ cup sugar.

5
Heat till just boiling.

6
Lower the heat and simmer for about 15 min.

7
Let cool, drain out the liquid, then pour the solids into a container.

8
Refrigerate overnight. Munch or store in the fridge for up to a week.

Pumpkin Butter

Makes 2 Cups

1
Remove the skin and seeds, then chop a small pumpkin.

2
Boil 2 cups of the pumpkin in water till soft.

3
Drain the water and toss the pumpkin into a blender.

4
Add a spoonful of cinnamon, a few sprinklings of ginger, 2 spoonfuls of maple syrup, a splash of vanilla extract, and a splash of almond milk.

5
Blend.

6
Let cool and drain out the liquid. Spoon the solids into a container.

7
Refrigerate overnight. Munch or store in the fridge for up to 2 weeks.

Seitan

ROB the GLOB
VITAL WHEAT GLUTEN

Sweeter than Sugar Co.
MOLASSES

spice box
ONION POWDER

spice cap
CUMIN

spice bowl
GARLIC SALT

Serves ⊙ ⊙ ⊙

Tips

- If you can squeeze water out of the dough in Step 3, add more flour.
- Add liquid smoke for a BBQ flavor, cayenne for a spicier flavor, or vegan beef bouillon for a heavier flavor.

1
Add 1 cup vital wheat gluten to a bowl with a few sprinklings of onion powder, garlic salt, and cumin.

2
Add 1 cup water and stir till it forms a dough.

3
Add 2 more spoonfuls of gluten and knead for about a minute.

4
Heat 3 cups water in a pot with a spoonful of molasses and a sprinkling of garlic salt.

5
When the water starts to boil, break off bite-sized pieces of the dough and drop into the pot.

6
Simmer till all the water is gone, 20-30 min.

7
Munch or store in the fridge for up to a week.

Sunflower Seed Spread

Makes 2 Cups

Tip
- Add fresh herbs, spices, and seasonings to get just the flavor you like.

1
Soak 2 cups sunflower seeds in warm water for at least 15 min.

2
Drain the sunflower seeds and toss in blender.

3
Add a spoonful of basil, 3 spoonfuls of vinegar, 3 cloves of garlic, 1 cup water, and ½ spoonful of salt to the blender.

4
Blend.

5
Munch or store in the fridge for up to a week.

Weed Olive Oil

Makes 2 Cups

Tips

- Wait about an hour after eating one spoonful to test the potency.
- Skip Steps 3-5 if you don't have foil or an oven, but extend Step 7 to at least an hour.
- If you have a thermometer, use it to make sure the oil stays around 240°F.
- Add seasonings to get the flavor you like.

1
Preheat oven to 240°F.

2
Loosely grind 14 grams (½ oz) of weed.

3
Place a sheet of foil on a baking sheet, then spread the weed out on the foil.

4
Fold the foil over and seal the edges, then bake on middle rack for 45 min.

5
Remove from the oven and let cool for 30 min. before opening the foil.

6
Heat 2 cups olive oil in a pot on very low heat.

7
Mix the weed into the oil and stir often for 30 min. Never let it simmer or boil.

8
Turn off the heat and let cool for at least an hour. Overnight is ok.

9
Strain into a container and store for up to 3 months.

Shelf Life

Veggie or Fruit	Countertop	Fridge	Sealed in Freezer
Acorn Squash	1 month	4 days chopped, cooked, and sealed	10 months cooked
Apples	1 week	1 month whole in crisper drawer	5 months
Avocados	3–4 days	1 week whole	2 months halved with lemon juice
Bananas	3–4 days hung	1 week in crisper drawer after ripe	3 months peeled or unpeeled
Basil	3–4 days in shade	1 week sealed in crisper drawer	4 months with stems removed
Beans (cooked)	Same day	4 days sealed with cooking water	6 months strained
Beets	1–2 days	1 month sealed in crisper drawer	10 months
Bell Peppers	1 week	1 month sealed in crisper drawer	10 months
Blueberries	Same day	1 week sealed	10 months
Broccoli	Same day	1–2 weeks sealed	10 months
Brussels Sprouts	3–4 days	2–3 weeks in crisper drawer	10 months
Butternut Squash	2 months	3 days chopped and sealed	10 months chopped
Cabbage	3–4 days	3 weeks whole	10 months
Cannabis	5 months	Not recommended	Only briefly if making hash
Cauliflower	Same day	2 weeks whole	10 months chopped
Carrots	Same day	2 months sealed with tops removed	6 months chopped
Celery	Same day	2 weeks sealed	10 months chopped
Chives	Same day	10 days sealed	6 months
Cilantro	Same day	1 week sealed	4 months
Collard Greens	Same day	5 days sealed in crisper drawer	10 months with stems removed
Corn	1–2 days	2 days with husks	10 months
Cucumbers	Same day	1–2 weeks in crisper drawer	10 months
Dates	2 months sealed	6–12 months sealed	2 years
Eggplants	1 week in shade	1 week sealed	6 months
Garlic	4 months	2–3 months whole	1 year whole
Grapefruits	1 week	1 month whole	10 months peeled
Green Beans	Same day	1 week sealed in crisper drawer	10 months with ends cut off
Green Onions	1–2 days	1 week sealed	6 months

All times are estimates and depend on the freshness of your produce.
In general, all of these foods will last longer in a cool room away from sunlight.

Veggie or Fruit	Countertop	Fridge	Sealed in Freezer
Jackfruit	2 days	5-7 days	2 months chopped
Jalapeños	2 days	2 weeks sealed	10 months
Kale	Same day	1 week sealed in crisper drawer	10 months
Leeks	Same day	1 week sealed	10 months
Lemons	1 week	3 weeks whole	3 months whole
Lentils (cooked)	Same day	4 days sealed	5 months
Lettuce	Same day	1 week sealed	6 months
Limes	1 week	3 weeks whole	3 months whole
Mangoes	2-5 days	5 days whole	10 months chopped
Mushrooms	Same day	1 week in paper bag	10 months
Onions, Yellow & Red	3 months	2 weeks, peeled and sealed	6 months chopped
Peaches	2 days	1 week sealed	10 months chopped
Pears	3 days	1-2 weeks sealed	10 months chopped
Pineapples	3 days	3 days chopped and sealed	10 months chopped
Plantains	4 days	1 week whole	10 months chopped
Potatoes	2-3 months	Not recommended	10 months chopped
Pumpkin	1 month	4 days chopped and sealed	10 months chopped
Radishes	Same day	2 weeks sealed, tops removed	10 months
Raspberries	Same day	1 week	10 months
Spaghetti Squash	2 months	4 days chopped and sealed	10 months cooked
Spinach	Same day	1 week sealed	10 months
Strawberries	Same day	1 week	10 months with tops removed
Sweet Potatoes	2 weeks	Not recommended	10 months chopped
Tomatoes	3-5 days	1 week sliced or chopped	2 months chopped
Tomatoes, Cherry	1 week	1 week sealed	3 months
Watermelon	2 weeks	1 week chopped and sealed	10 months chopped
Yams	2 weeks	Not recommended	10 months chopped
Zucchini	Same day	3 days in crisper drawer	10 months chopped

Index

Text, illustrations, and photographs copyright © 2021 by Sarah Conrique and Graham I. Haynes

Published in the United States by Ten Speed Press, an imprint of Random House, a division of Penguin Random House LLC, New York.

www.tenspeed.com

Ten Speed Press and the Ten Speed Press colophon are registered trademarks of Penguin Random House LLC.

Some of these recipes originally appeared on the authors' website, www.theveganstoner.com.

Design by Simple Gestures Design Studio.

Library of Congress Control Number: 2020943119

Hardcover ISBN: 978-1-9848-5845-0
eBook ISBN: 978-1-9848-5846-7

Printed in China

10 9 8 7 6 5 4 3 2 1

First Edition

Volume

U.S.	Imperial	Metric
1 tablespoon	½ fl oz	15 ml
2 tablespoons	1 fl oz	30 ml
¼ cup	2 fl oz	60 ml
⅓ cup	3 fl oz	90 ml
½ cup	4 fl oz	120 ml
⅔ cup	5 fl oz (¼ pint)	150 ml
¾ cup	6 fl oz	180 ml
1 cup	8 fl oz (⅓ pint)	240 ml
1¼ cups	10 fl oz (½ pint)	300 ml
2 cups (1 pint)	16 fl oz (⅔ pint)	480 ml
2½ cups	20 fl oz (1 pint)	600 ml
1 quart	32 fl oz (1⅔ pints)	1 l

Temperature

Fahrenheit	Celsius/Gas Mark
250°F	120°C/gas mark ½
275°F	135°C/gas mark 1
300°F	150°C/gas mark 2
325°F	160°C/gas mark 3
350°F	175 or 180°C/gas mark 4
375°F	190°C/gas mark 5
400°F	200°C/gas mark 6
425°F	220°C/gas mark 7
450°F	230°C/gas mark 8
475°F	245°C/gas mark 9
500°F	260°C

Length

Inch	Metric
¼ inch	6 mm
½ inch	1.25 cm
¾ inch	2 cm
1 inch	2.5 cm
6 inches	15 cm
12 inches	30 cm

Weight

U.S./Imperial	Metric
½ oz	15 g
1 oz	30 g
2 oz	60 g
¼ lb	115 g
⅓ lb	150 g
½ lb	225 g
¾ lb	350 g
1 lb	450 g

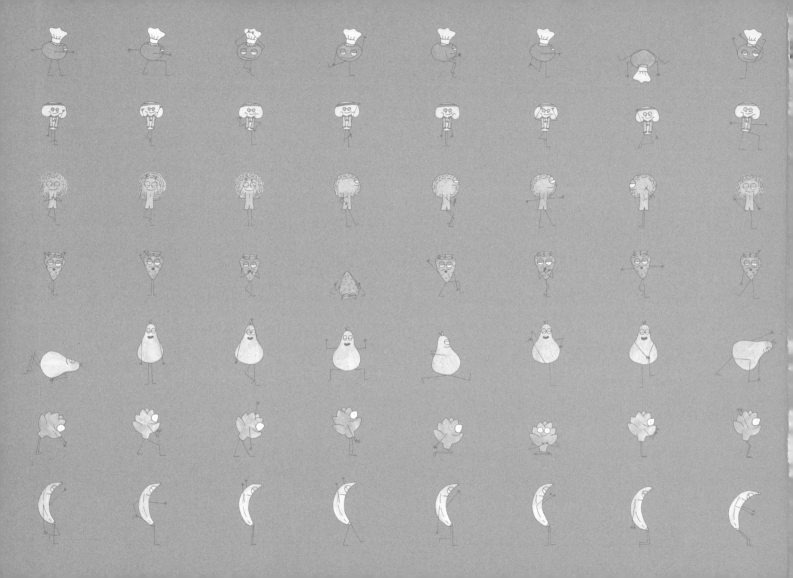